# PROFESSOR COOK'S SMASHING SNACKS

**Enslow Publishers, Inc.**
40 Industrial Road
Box 398
Berkeley Heights, NJ 07922
USA
http://www.enslow.com

This edition published by Enslow Publishers Inc.

**Library of Congress Cataloging-in-Publication Data:**

Brash, Lorna.
  Professor Cook's Smashing Snacks / Lorna Brash.
    pages cm. — (Professor Cook's ...)
  Audience: 9-12
  Audience: Grade 4 to Grade 6
  Summary: "A variety of snacks for kids to make, and science facts explaining how ingredients react with each other"—Provided by publisher.
  Includes bibliographical references.
  ISBN 978-0-7660-4304-6
  1. Snack foods—Juvenile literature. 2. Coooking—Juvenile literature.  I. Title. II. Series.
  TX740.S374 2013
  641.5'3—dc23

2012031118

Future edition:
        Paperback ISBN: 978-1-4644-0553-2

**To Our Readers:**
We have done our best to make sure all Internet addresses in this book were active and appropriate when we went to press. However, the author and the publisher have no control over and assume no liability for the material available on those Internet sites or on other Web sites they may link to. Any comments or suggestions can be sent by e-mail to comments@enslow.com or to the address on the back cover.

Printed in China

012013 WKT, Shenzhen, Guangdong, China

10 9 8 7 6 5 4 3 2 1

First published in the UK in 2012 by Wayland

Copyright © Wayland 2012

Wayland
338 Euston Rd
London NW1 3BH

Editor: Debbie Foy
Designer: Lisa Peacock
Photographer: Ian Garlick
Proofreader/indexer: Sarah Doughty
Consultant: Sean Connolly

Wayland is a division of Hachette Children's Books, an Hachette UK company.
www.hachette.co.uk

# Contents

# PROFESSOR COOK'S... INCREDIBLE EDIBLES

**Are you hungry to learn more about your food?**

Have you ever wondered why some foods behave the way they do? For example, have you ever looked closely at popcorn and wondered how your puffy, chewy snack started life as a hard yellow seed?

Or, have you ever bitten into a toasted sandwich and wondered how that once-rubbery ball of mozzarella has transformed into an impressively soft and stringy, goo-ey cheese?

Find out the answers to these questions and more by joining Professor Cook's team to make instant ice cream in a bag, onion bhajis without the tears, or try your hand at "glassy" caramel shards to totally pep up your ice cream!

Happy ~~Experimenting~~ Cooking!

# PROFESSOR COOK'S KITCHEN RULE BOOK

→ Wash your hands before you start cooking and after handling raw stuff, like meat

→ Mop up spills as soon as they happen

→ Use oven gloves for handling hot dishes straight from the oven

→ Take care with sharp knives. Don't walk around with them!

→ Turn off the oven or stovetop when you have finished cooking

→ Use separate cutting boards for vegetables and meat

→ Raw and cooked foods should be kept separate in the fridge

→ Don't forget to tidy up the kitchen afterwards! No-brainer, huh?

## ABBREVIATIONS

c = cup

tsp = teaspoon

tbsp = tablespoon

oz = ounce

°F = degrees Fahrenheit

HOT GOODS!

WHEN YOU SEE THIS WARNING SIGN AN ADULT'S HELP MAY BE NEEDED!

# The "Science Bits"

Believe it or not, cooking involves a lot of science! The Science Bits that accompany each of Professor Cook's delicious recipes answer all the mysteries about food that you have ever wondered about. They also explore some of the interesting, unusual or downright quirky ways that our food can often behave!

# POP-TASTIC POPCORN

Have you ever wondered how a tiny, hard seed explodes to nearly 40 times its original size, and becomes a yummy snack? Sweet or salty, popcorn is the perfect cinema treat, but our combination of spices leaves you with a really deliciously pop-tastic snack for any time of day!

## Stuff you need:

2 tbsp corn oil
2 1/2 oz popcorn kernels
1 tbsp salted butter
1 garlic clove, crushed
1 tsp curry powder
1/2 tsp mild chili powder
1/4 tsp fine table salt

Serves 6

HOT GOODS!

## Step 1

Place the oil into a medium-sized saucepan and heat until the oil is hot but not smoking.

## Step 2

Add the popcorn kernels and stir. Cover with a tight-fitting lid and place over a high heat, holding the lid firmly in place and shaking the pan occasionally. You will hear the corn pop!

Popcorn kernels have been known to pop up to 35 inches into the air!

## Step 3

In a separate pan, melt the butter until foaming, then add the garlic, curry, and chili powders and cook for 30 seconds, stirring with a wooden spoon.

## The Science Bit

### How does popcorn pop?

When the popcorn kernels are heated in the pan, the trapped moisture inside them expands and turns into steam. The buildup of steam is so intense that it bursts through the hard outer shell and the starch inside the kernel explodes, literally turning it inside out! The soft starch expands and puffs up to form the fluffy, yummy corn snack that we all love!

## Step 4

Add the popped corn to the butter mixture and stir well. Place it into a bowl, sprinkle with salt, and toss the popcorn with your hands until well mixed.

## Stuff you need:

Nonstick Teflon mat
1 c superfine sugar
5 1/3 oz golden syrup
3 1/2 oz salted peanuts
1 3/4 oz shelled pistachio
nuts, roughly chopped
4 tbsp sesame seeds
1 tsp vanilla extract
1 3/4 tbsp softened butter
1 tsp baking soda

Serves 6-8

**HOT GOODS!**

## The Science Bit

### How does sugar become brittle, just like glass?

When sugar is heated, the sugar crystals (that are arranged
in the clever little 3D granules you can see in your sugar
bowl) break down. As they cool, the sugar molecules join
up, but they are no longer crystals. This means that light
can now appear through the gaps in the molecules,
making the shards transparent, and able to shatter,
just like glass!

# SMASHING CARAMEL SHARDS

These brittle shards of caramel with healthy nuts and seeds crackle and crunch in your mouth. Smash with a rolling pin and scatter over your favorite ice cream!

## Step 1

Line a large baking sheet with a nonstick Teflon mat.

## Step 2

Put the sugar, 1/4 c water, and golden syrup into a heavy based saucepan. Gently heat and stir until the sugar has dissolved. Bring to a gentle boil for 4–5 minutes until the mixture turns a pale toffee color. Take care — the mixture will be very hot!

## Step 3

Quickly add the nuts, seeds, vanilla, butter, and baking soda and blend until the butter has melted and the mixture is well combined.

## Step 4

Quickly pour onto the nonstick mat. Leave to cool for at least 25 minutes before breaking into shards.

# ICE CREAM IN A BAG!

**D**id you know that it's possible to make ice cream without a freezer? Follow our fun recipe to create delicious vanilla ice cream — all through the marvellous magic of science!

## Stuff you need:

1/2 c whole milk

1 tbsp sugar

1/2 tsp vanilla extract

Pint-sized resealable freezer bag

Quart-sized resealable freezer bag

6 tbsp salt

21 ice cubes

A pair of woolly gloves!

Serves 1

## Step 1

In a measuring cup, mix together the milk, sugar, and vanilla, then pour the mixture into the pint-sized resealable freezer bag and seal tightly. Set aside.

## Step 2

Place the salt and ice cubes into the quart-sized resealable freezer bag. Place the smaller bag inside the larger one so that the two sealed edges are near each other.

## The Science Bit

### How do you make ice cream without a freezer?

Easy-peasy! Salt lowers the freezing point of ice, causing it to melt. And when something melts, it absorbs heat energy from something else (in this case, the cream mixture). So, the cream loses heat (gets colder) until it begins to freeze. Shaking the bag stops it from freezing into one big block. Instead it creates tiny ice crystals in the milk fat, which in turn creates your deliciously creamy ice cream!

## Step 3

Put on your cozy gloves! Hold the two zip-locked sealed edges together and with both hands shake the bags for 8-10 minutes until you feel the milk mixture thicken to an ice cream.

## Step 4

Remove the smaller bag from the larger bag. Wipe the bag to remove the salt (as you don't want salty ice cream — yuk!), but don't run it under the cold tap or your ice cream will melt. Squeeze the ice cream into a bowl, top with your favorite fruit, and eat right away!

## Stuff you need:

1 3/4 tbsp butter, softened
2 slices brown bread
2 slices honey roast ham
2 3/4 oz mozzarella cheese,
   thinly sliced
1 ripe tomato, sliced
Basil leaves
Salt and black pepper

Serves 1

# The Science Bit

## Why is mozzarella so stretchy?

Mozzarella is cool. You can bounce it like rubber, stretch it like elastic, and melt it like plastic. Not many cheeses do all of that! When mozzarella is made, a mild acid (such as citric acid) is added to make the milk curdle. It is this combination of acid and heat that makes the texture of this cheese so stringy and elastic. The cheese curds are stretched and kneaded until smooth, and then they are formed into round balls as fresh mozzarella cheese!

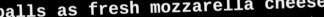

# CHEESE-AND-HAM-O-RAMA!

**C**risp and toasty on the outside and ooey-gooey cheese on the inside. Serve with a green salad and a big dollop of ketchup for a finger-licking treat!

## Step 1

Butter each slice of bread. Top one slice of bread with a piece of ham. Then add the mozzarella, sliced tomato, and basil leaves. Season with salt and freshly ground black pepper. Finally add another slice of ham and then sandwich together with the remaining slice of bread.

## Step 2

Preheat the grill to hot. Place the sandwich on a baking sheet and press to compact it slightly. Grill on the middle shelf for about 3 minutes or until the bread is golden.

## Step 3

Carefully turn the sandwich over and grill for a further 3 minutes until bubbling and golden. Cut in half and serve.

# HOMEMADE BEANS ON TOAST

Baked beans are often best known for their hilarious aftereffects, but in fact they are packed full of protein, fiber, vitamins, and minerals. If they are that good, we thought we'd better find out how to make our own amazing version!

## Stuff you need:

2 tbsp olive oil
2 red onions, finely chopped
5 1/3 oz streaky bacon, finely chopped
2 garlic cloves, crushed
14 oz can chopped tomatoes
2 tbsp dark brown sugar
1 tbsp Worcestershire sauce
2 x 14 oz cans navy beans
Salt and black pepper
4 slices crusty brown bread
1 tbsp butter
1 3/4 oz Cheddar cheese, coarsely grated

Serves 4

## Step 1

Add the oil to the saucepan and fry the onions and bacon for 8 minutes, stirring occasionally until softened. Add in the garlic, tomatoes, sugar, and Worcestershire sauce. Bring to a boil, then reduce the heat to low, cover, and cook for 20 minutes stirring occasionally until the sauce is thickened. Whiz with a hand blender until the sauce is thick.

## Step 2

Drain the beans and stir them into the tomato sauce. Simmer for 5–10 minutes until warmed through. Season to taste with salt and freshly ground black pepper. Keep warm.

## Step 3

Toast the bread until golden brown, and spread with butter. Spoon some of the beans over the toast. Sprinkle with grated cheese to serve.

## The Science Bit

### Why do beans give you gas?

It's simple. Beans are very high in fiber, which is not easily broken down by our digestive systems. The partially broken down food passes farther through the gut to the large intestine where it is further broken down creating carbon dioxide ($CO_2$) and other gases! We have used canned beans in this recipe, but if you are using dried beans, try soaking them overnight before cooking as this can help to break down the indigestible sugars that cause these noisy symptoms!

## Stuff you need:

1/2 c softened unsalted butter
1/2 c superfine sugar
1 egg
1 tsp vanilla extract
4 1/2 oz steel-cut oats
1 1/4 c plain flour
1/2 tsp baking powder
4 1/2 oz white chocolate, chopped
4 1/2 oz plain dark chocolate, chopped

Makes 16 cookies

These cookies are a great mid-morning snack as the oats fill up your tummy for longer! Serve them with a fresh fruit berry smoothie.

## Step 1

Preheat the oven to 350°F. Line two baking sheets with nonstick baking parchment. Beat the butter and superfine sugar in a mixing bowl with a wooden spoon until creamy. Break in the egg and add the vanilla and oats and stir until mixed.

16

# OAT-SO YUMMY POWER COOKIE

## Step 2

Sift over the flour and baking powder and stir in the chopped chocolate until all the ingredients are well mixed together.

## Step 3

Drop 16 teaspoonfuls of the cookie mixture, evenly spaced apart, onto the prepared baking sheets.

## Step 4

Flatten slightly with the back of a fork. Bake for 12–15 minutes until risen slightly and golden. Transfer to a cooling rack to cool completely. Store in an airtight container and eat within 1 week.

## The Science Bit

### Why are oats so good to eat in the morning?

Oats contain bags of fiber, which adds bulk to your digestive system and slows down the digestive process. The body breaks down and burns fiber a lot slower than it does most other foods, so this makes you feel fuller for longer. The equation is: Feeling Full + Fewer Snacks = Healthier Diet!

17

# "NO-CRY" ONION BHAJIS & DIP

Try these utterly spice-tastic "no-cry" onion bhajis for a light and delicious snack. Goggles are an unusual ingredient here...!

## Stuff you need:

For the dip:
1 1/2 in piece cucumber
2 tomatoes
5 oz Greek yogurt
Fresh coriander, chopped
Salt and black pepper

For the bhajis:
2 c gram flour
1 tsp mild chili powder
1 tsp ground turmeric
1 tsp ground coriander
1 tsp ground cumin
1/2 tsp salt
A pair of goggles
3 large Spanish onions
Sunflower oil, for frying

Serves 4

HOT GOODS!

## Step 1

For the dip, finely chop the cucumber and tomatoes. Stir both into the yogurt along with the fresh coriander. Season with salt and pepper.

## Step 2

Place the gram flour, chili powder, turmeric, ground coriander, cumin, and salt into a large mixing bowl. Gradually whisk in 1 1/4 c water to make a smooth thick batter. Now pop on your goggles! Slice the onions and separate into rings.

goggles

18

Onions are thought to act as an anti-inflammatory, and so are often used to soothe insect stings!

## The Science Bit

### Why do onions make you cry?

When you slice through an onion, sulphenic acids are released, which mix with enzymes in the onion to produce a gas. This gas combines with the tears in your eyes to create a mild form of sulphuric acid, which irritates the surface of the eye. The eye's defense mechanism is to produce tears to wash away the irritation, but by wearing goggles, you are preventing the gas from getting into your eyes and making you cry!

## Step 3

Place the individual onion rings into the batter and stir well until all the onions are covered in batter.

## Step 4

Pour 3/4 in of oil into a deep frying pan and heat until a piece of bread turns golden in 20 seconds. Place spoonfuls of the onion mixture into the oil and cook for 3 minutes, turning half way through, until crispy and golden. Remove with a slotted spoon and drain on paper towels. Serve with the cool yogurt dip!

# DOUBLE-DIPPED MALLOW COOKIES

D o you like math? Here's a simple sum for you: fluffy marshmallows + graham crackers + chocolate + toasted coconut = cookie heaven!

## Step 1

Place 4 pink marshmallows into the center of 4 of the graham crackers and 4 white marshmallows into the center of another 4 graham crackers. Place one cracker and marshmallow onto a plate and heat in a microwave for about 10 seconds. You will see the marshmallow "explode" and double in size.

## Step 2

Immediately use one of the plain crackers to make a "sandwich" by pressing the two crackers together gently. Set aside and cook the remaining crackers and marshmallows until you have 8 cookie sandwiches.

## Step 3

Break the
chocolate into
pieces, place it
in a heatproof
bowl and allow
to melt over a
saucepan of
simmering water. Carefully remove
the bowl from the saucepan. Place
the chocolate into one dish and the
coconut into another. Half dip
the cookies into the chocolate
and then the toasted coconut.

## Step 4

Place the
cookies on a
baking tray
lined with baking
parchment. Allow
to set completely.
Store in an airtight
container.

## The Science Bit

### Can chocolate really make us feel good?

Of course chocolate makes
us feel good, right? But
in fact, recent scientific
research has actually
proved it! Apparently,
eating chocolate can
cause the brain to
release endorphins,
which are chemicals that
circulate in our blood to
make us feel great!
How cool is that?
Bring on the chocolate!

# MINI SUPERHERO PIES!

These crisp mini pies are filled with tangy feta cheese, "superfood" spinach, and deliciously crunchy pine nuts. A great combination of healthy stuff with a tantalizing texture!

## Stuff you need:

7 oz baby spinach leaves
5 1/3 oz feta cheese, crumbled
4 tbsp toasted pine nuts
Handful chopped mint and parsley
2 tbsp beaten egg
Salt and black pepper
9 1/2 oz filo pastry sheets
3 1/2 tbsp butter, melted

Makes 18 pies

## Step 1

Preheat the oven to 375°F. Wash the spinach and drain any excess water. Put it in a saucepan with only the water that is clinging to the leaves and place over a low heat until the spinach has wilted. Allow to cool.

## Step 2

Stir the cheese, pine nuts, mint, parsley, and beaten egg into the spinach and stir well to combine. Season with salt and black pepper.

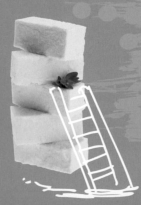

## Step 3

Cut the filo dough sheets lengthways into three long, thin strips of an equal size. Cover two bundles of dough strips with a clean dish towel to prevent them from drying out. Lift off two thin strips of filo dough and brush each of them with melted butter. Cover each with another (unbuttered) dough strip.

## Step 4

Place a teaspoonful of the spinach filling at the bottom of the pastry strip. Lift the bottom right corner over the spinach to produce a triangle shape. Continue to flip the filled triangle over to create a triangular shape down the length of the filo strip. Repeat until you have used all the butter, dough and spinach filling.

## Step 5

Brush the mini pies with butter and bake for 20 minutes until golden brown.

## The Science Bit

### Do pine nuts come from pine trees?

Believe it or not, yes! Pine nuts are an edible seed that are found inside pinecones. They are also the main ingredient of pesto sauce. They have a high fat content and so to bring out their flavor it's a good idea to "toast" them in a frying pan without oil.

23

# GOLD BULLION HONEYCOMB BARS!

These bullion bars packed with crunchy honeycomb are pure gold (well, almost!). Keep them locked up in an airtight treasure chest (or plastic container) or they won't be around for long!

## Step 1

Wet the insides of 8 mini loaf pans (or an 8-in square cake pan if you don't have the mini version) with water. Then line the base and sides of the pans with plastic wrap.

## Step 2

Break the chocolate into squares and place in a heatproof bowl with the butter. Melt over a pan of simmering water until nice and runny. Then carefully remove the bowl from the heat.

24

# Step 3

Stir the hazelnuts, crushed honeycomb bars, graham crackers, and raisins into the runny chocolate.

Fill each pan with the mixture and level the surface. Leave to chill in the fridge for 45 minutes.

# Step 4

Turn the chocolate mixture out of the pans by giving them a hard knock on a work surface. Remove the plastic wrap. Wrap each bullion bar in gold paper and dust with gold glitter!

## The Science Bit

### Who or what is responsible for the holes in honeycomb?

Well, first off, the honeycomb that we've used in this recipe needs really high heat to make, which is why we have used store-bought bars, but it is worth looking a little more closely at honeycomb with its wholly holey texture...
When baking soda (an ingredient that helps mixtures rise) is heated with sugar syrup, oodles of carbon dioxide ($CO_2$) gas are released. It is this $CO_2$ that permeates the sugar mixture, creating the lovely bubbly melt-on-your-tongue texture of honeycomb!

Different chemical taste detectors on parts of your tongue are programmed to detect the acidity of the sour lemons or the sweetness of the sugar!

# The Science Bit

## So what makes the fizz?

The baking soda reacts with the acid in the lemons and the sugar to form carbon dioxide ($CO_2$) gas. This gas is released in millions of small fizzy bubbles that rise to the surface of the lemonade to try to escape!

# PINK FIZZBOMB LEMONADE

Try this fruity and refreshing drink with a cool tongue-tingling effect as the bubbles get busy!

## Step 1

Cut each lemon into about 8 wedges. Remove any seeds and place into a food processor or blender. Add half the superfine sugar, the crushed ice, and 2 c water. Blend to a puree.

## Step 2

Place a sieve over a large bowl and pour the lemon mixture in. Sieve to remove the pith. Take the pith back to the food processor with the remaining superfine sugar, raspberries, and another 2 c water and whiz again. Sieve into the previous lemon mixture. Discard anything left in the sieve.

## Step 3

Mix together the citric acid, baking soda, and confectioner's sugar. Place a heaped teaspoonful into the bottom of a glass and pour over the lemon mixture. Give it a good stir and drink.

**For the bread sticks:**
1 1/2 c strong plain bread flour, plus extra for dusting
1/2 tsp superfine sugar
1/2 tsp coarse sea salt
1/2 tsp instant yeast
2 tbsp olive oil, plus extra for oiling

**For the dip:**
2 tbsp sour cream
2 tbsp mayonnaise
1 3/4 oz Cheddar cheese, coarsely grated
1 spring onion, finely chopped
Pinch of cayenne pepper

Makes 12 bread sticks (and enough dip for 4 people)

What makes all those tiny holes in bread? Has something been eating it before you? Yeast is the stuff that makes bread rise —but what is it? And how does it work?

## Step 1

Mix the flour, sugar, salt, and yeast into a large bowl. Make a well in the center and pour in the olive oil and 1/2 c water (make sure the water is not boiling, just hand hot). Mix to a soft dough.

# BIG DIPPER BREAD STICKS

## Step 2

Knead the dough for 8–10 minutes until it is smooth and elastic. Oil your mixing bowl and place the dough back into the bowl. Cover with a clean dish towel and leave to rise for 10 minutes.

## Step 3

Cut the dough into 12 equal pieces and roll each into a long, thin stick about 10 in long. Sprinkle a little flour over two baking sheets and arrange the bread sticks evenly on the baking sheets. Leave to rise in a warm place for 45 minutes until doubled in size.

## Step 4

Preheat the oven to 400°F. Bake the bread sticks for 18-20 minutes until golden. Mix together all the dip ingredients until well combined. Spoon into a bowl and dip in!

## The Science Bit
### What is yeast and how does it work?

Believe it or not, yeast is a living fungi that converts the natural sugars in flour into carbon dioxide ($CO_2$). This gas is the cause of all the tiny little bubbles you can see in bread! Without yeast our bread would be hard and flat. With yeast, a small amount of sugar for it to feed on, warmth, and a good kneading, your homemade bread (or bread sticks) will have a delicious, soft texture.

**ANTI-INFLAMMATORY** a substance that can reduce swelling or irritation to the skin

**BAKING SODA** a soluble white powder mainly used in fizzy drinks and as a rising agent in baking

**BEAT** a quick and vigorous mix with a spoon or whisk

**BLEND** to mix two or more ingredients together

**CITRIC ACID** a sharp-tasting acid that is found in lemons and other citrus fruits

**CORIANDER** a herb widely used in Asian cooking

**CUMIN** a pungent spice often used in Indian cooking

**CURDS** when milk is being made into cheese, the solid parts of the cheese are known as curds

**EDIBLE** something that is fit to be eaten

**ENDORPHINS** chemicals that can act on the brain to make us feel happy

**ENZYMES** substances that are found in our food. Their job is to speed up natural processes

**FILO DOUGH** a wafer-thin pastry made from unleavened flour dough

**FRY** to cook food with oil in a shallow frying pan

**FUNGI** the name given to a group of living things, which includes yeast for making bread. The group also includes mushrooms

**GRAM FLOUR** a flour made from ground chickpeas often used in Indian cooking

KERNEL the seed or hard husk of a cereal, such as wheat

KNEAD to fold, push, and pull dough with your hands until it becomes soft and smooth

LARGE INTESTINE the lower part of the bowel that absorbs water from food and gets rid of waste products

MOLECULES the smallest units of a chemical substance or compound

SIEVE to strain a liquid or push something through a sieve to get rid of lumps

SIMMER to cook at just below boiling point, bubbling gently

SUPERFOODS nutrient-rich foods that can help to fight off aging and illness.

TURMERIC a bright yellow spice used mainly in Indian and Asian cooking

WHISK to mix something quickly to get air into it

YEAST an agent used to rise dough in bread making

# INDEX

# USEFUL WEB SITES

**www.spatulatta.com**
Get some basic cooking skills under your belt, with step-by-step video recipes and a recipe box that includes options for cooking a meal by choosing a basic ingredient, a type of food, occasion, or particular diet.

**www.yummyscience.co.uk**
Super-fun science projects to try out in the kitchen using everyday foods. Grow your own crystals with salt, test out the toasting properties of bread, or make your own honeycomb toffee. Some of these recipes call for an adult's help, so always make sure you let an adult know before you start.

**www.exploratorium.edu/cooking**
Find out how a pinch of curiosity can improve your cooking! Explore recipes, activities, and webcasts that will improve your understanding of the science behind food and cooking.